Composing Photographs

Read *Composing Photographs* and learn
how to—

- Recognize and implement the elements of
  composition.

- Make subjects look three-dimensional within
  a two-dimensional image.

- Frame a subject to give it dramatic impact.

- Develop your own personal style.

THE NO NONSENSE LIBRARY

OTHER NO NONSENSE PHOTOGRAPHY GUIDES

Photographing People
Photographing Your Vacation
Using Accessory Equipment
Using Creative Techniques
Using Existing Light

OTHER NO NONSENSE GUIDES

Car Guides
Career Guides
Cooking Guides
Financial Guides
Health Guides
Legal Guides
Parenting Guides
Real Estate Guides
Study Guides
Success Guides
Wine Guides

NO NONSENSE PHOTOGRAPHY GUIDE™

COMPOSING PHOTOGRAPHS

A KODAK Book

ROBERT HERKO

Longmeadow Press

COMPOSING PHOTOGRAPHS

Published by Longmeadow Press, 201 High Ridge Road, Stamford, Connecticut 06904. No part of this book may be reproduced or used in any form or by any means, electronic or mechanical, including photocopying, recording, or by an information storage and retrieval system, without permission in writing from the publisher.

No Nonsense Photography Guide is a trademark controlled by Longmeadow Press.

ISBN 0-681-40730-1

Copyright © 1990 by The Image Bank, Inc.

Produced by The Image Bank in association with Eastman Kodak Company, Rochester, New York.

Kodak is a registered trademark of Eastman Kodak Company and is used under license from Kodak.

The Image Bank® is a registered trademark of The Image Bank, Inc.

Printed in Spain

0 9 8 7 6 5 4 3 2 1

Producer: Solomon M. Skolnick; *Managing Editor:* Elizabeth Loonan; *Editors:* Terri Hardin (The Image Bank), Margaret Buckley (Kodak), Derek Doeffinger (Kodak); *Production Director:* Charles W. Styles (Kodak); *Production Coordinator:* Ann-Louise Lipman (The Image Bank); *Editorial Assistant:* Carol Raguso; *Production Assistant:* Valerie Zars; *Photo Researchers:* Natalie Goldstein, Lenore Weber; *Copy Editor:* Irene S. Korn; *Art Direction and Design:* Chase/Temkin & Associates, Inc.

Cover photographs, left to right: Richard and Mary Magruder, Larry Dale Gordon, Bill Varie

For information about the photographs in this book, please contact:
The Image Bank
111 Fifth Avenue
New York, N.Y. 10003

TABLE OF CONTENTS

INTRODUCTION

Composition encompasses many aspects of how photographs appear. Understanding and using composition is the basic difference between the amateur and professional photographer. For example, the amateur photographer may take a quick snapshot without considering how the photograph will appear; the professional, however, thinks about subject placement, lighting, viewpoint and perspective—all part of composition.

There are no hard-and-fast rules for good composition—merely guidelines to help you build better photographs. These guidelines do not apply to every situation. If you adhere to "formulas," not only will your photos be repetitious but you will ignore many wonderful subjects that stray from the formulas. To compose great photographs, you must recognize and respond to subjects in your own style. In short, you must learn to inject your personality into your photos.

Many people believe you need expensive camera equipment to make eye-catching photographs. Not so. Although the single-lens-reflex (SLR) camera is mentioned throughout this book, it is equally important to have an alert eye and a mind willing to manipulate it. If you cultivate these, your photos will surpass even those made by photographers who have thousands of dollars' worth of lenses and cameras but have only nickle-and-dime responses to scenes. With the ability to "see" your subject—rather than just "look" at it—you can visualize how it will appear in the photo.

Composing Photographs will show you how to ferret out the uncommon aspects of ordinary subjects and compose unusual subjects to create appealing photographs. You will learn how to use your equipment to accentuate or even exaggerate a subject's unique features. To help you understand, some key photographic terms are in italics—these can be found in the glossary at the back of the book.

Most of all, you will learn to judge how a subject will appear in a photograph and to examine what you are photographing, so that you effectively communicate your feelings about the people, places, and events in your life.

THE ELEMENTS OF
COMPOSITION

Charles Mahaux

Good composition combines the artistic with the technical to create attention-grabbing photographs. No two people approach the same subject in the same way; that is why two photographers at the same scene and with identical cameras will not take the same picture. Your personal composition—the manner in which you structure and interpret the subject—determines how effectively your photograph communicates.

Clarity and simplicity are the keys to good composition. Photographs cluttered with irrelevant subject matter seem pointless and disorganized. Remember that the eye and the mind wish to perceive all things with order. Lack of order will confuse the viewer, and what you intend to be seen may be lost.

It's surprising how often simple things are overlooked, only to crop up in the final image and ruin the effect of your composition. For example, plastic bags, carelessly tossed in a corner, will interrupt the straight line of the floor, and rumpled coats in the background will distract the viewer with their indistinct shapes and bright colors.

It is important that you be aware of your composition as a whole and not just concentrate on your subject. Ask yourself these questions just before you make a photograph: Have I really looked at the scene I am about to shoot? Is there anything in the background that will detract from my subject?

The primary visual elements are lines, shapes, contrasts, forms, textures, and, in color photography, hues. The placement and arrangement of these primary visual elements within the frame permit the photographer to represent three-dimensional reality within the confines of a two-dimensional photo. Secondary elements such as image sharpness, perspective relationship, timing (with subjects in motion), visual balance and implied dynamics also figure in the composition of your photograph.

Part One will acquaint you with the importance of subject placement (including the very useful "rule of thirds"), the strength of color, and the meaning and use of lines. Part One also discusses the roles that shape and form, pattern and texture, and the properties of light play in composing photographs.

ELEMENTS OF COMPOSITION

SUBJECT PLACEMENT

Where you place your subject in the photographic frame is crucial to the overall success of your composition; it tells the viewer not only what you consider important in the photograph, but also how you feel about what you are photographing.

Subject placement breaks into two categories, centered and off-center subjects, and is addressed by the rule of thirds.

Centered subjects. The most basic aspect of composition is where you position the subject in the picture. Many photographers place the subject dead center in the picture because the focusing circle or autofocus target is in the center of the viewfinder. The weak symmetry created by placing a typical subject in the center of the frame makes a very static photograph. Although a centered subject commands attention, the space surrounding the subject often fails to support it. Place a subject in the center of the picture only if the subject shows strong symmetry itself. The spokes radiating from a bike wheel, the grille

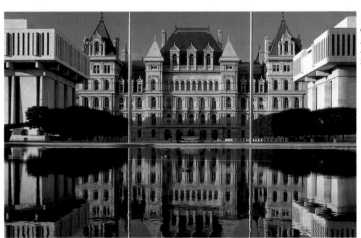

Nicholas Foster

This photograph is practically a kaleidoscope of symmetry, with the main entrance of the building centered between two poles, and the whole scene mirrored in the water.

COMPOSING PHOTOGRAPHS

of a '52 De Soto, the reflection of a mountain in a lake—all show a strong symmetry that will be reinforced by being centered in a picture.

Effective positioning of lines and shapes lends a feeling of motion or dynamics to a centered subject. The subject may include strategic points or features located off-center that command attention and lead the viewer's eye away from the center of the frame.

Lou Jones

Grant V. Faint

At the top, the weight lifter hoists bar bells in a dynamic, frame-filling pose. Below, the photograph of the child sitting in the middle of a pumpkin field tells a colorful and interesting story.

Inone/Grimberg

Inone/Grimberg

While centering the subject is a natural choice, placing the subject off-center can also be interesting.

Off-center subjects. More often you can create dynamic and interesting compositions by locating the principal subject away from the center of the frame. The asymmetrical division of space within the image allows you to insert other dynamic elements. Dividing a frame in this manner also lets you create dynamic relationships between the foreground and background; it makes better use of perspective, since the environment of the subject can be more effectively employed.

COMPOSING PHOTOGRAPHS

If you have an autofocus camera and your photos of off-center subjects look out of focus, review the focusing procedure in your camera manual. Most autofocus cameras focus on whatever is in the center of the viewfinder. To retain focus on off-center subjects, you will need to use the focus lock on your camera.

Eric L. Wheater

In the top photograph, a child peeps charmingly out of a window in an off-center portrait, while below, the leanness of the man matches the rows of pillars to his right.

Marc Romanelli

ELEMENTS OF COMPOSITION

The rule of thirds helps determine the placement of off-center subjects. Here, the near balloon and the cluster of distant ones appear at intersecting points formed by the rule's imaginary grid.

The rule of thirds. An excellent starting point for subject placement is the "rule of thirds." According to the rule of thirds, you should locate the strongest visual points in a frame by dividing the entire frame into three equal sections both vertically and horizontally (like a tic-tac-toe grid). You then place the subject at one of the four intersections to build a strong composition. Placement of subjects at one of the four intersections seems to please the mind. You can make a compelling portrait by placing either the right or left eye of your subject at one of these intersections. The rule of thirds applies whether you hold the camera vertically or horizontally.

One note of caution: If you constantly place subjects at one of these points, some of your photographs may look monotonous.

COMPOSING PHOTOGRAPHS

Michael Rosenfeld/G+J Images

You can use the rule of thirds in many creative ways. At the top, notice the symmetry of the father and son's eyes along the top "latitudinal" line, and each balloon at a "longitudinal" line. Lower, the mother's face appears at the intersection.

Butch Martin

ELEMENTS OF COMPOSITION

THE STRENGTH OF COLOR

Color in itself has an inherent brightness that affects how a scene is perceived. In a scene with equal intensities of yellow and blue, the yellow will always appear brighter. Red stripes on a field of blue will always appear harsh, because our eyes have trouble resolving two contrasting colors simultaneously and

Paolo Curto

In these photographs, note how yellows and reds advance from the "cooler" blues.

Eric L. Wheater

COMPOSING PHOTOGRAPHS

Cool colors, such as greens, recede, while yellows pop out of the picture. The visual strength of yellow makes it a strong compositional tool, as in the photograph below.

David Muench

Robert Farber

jump back and forth between the two. In general, we tend to perceive warm colors such as yellow, orange, and red as advancing from the plane of the photograph, appearing closer to us, and cool colors such as blues and greens as receding from our eyes. By composing a photo so that warm colors are in the foreground and cool colors in the background, you can emphasize depth.

With color filters, you can manipulate the colors of a scene to alter the mood. Colored filters come in a variety of colors and densities. You can subtly warm up a scene with an amber No. 81C filter or subtly cool it with a blue No. 82A filter. Or you can make moody monochromes with deep-colored filters that transform a scene into a single color. A blue No. 47 filter will give a daylight seascape a moonlight effect. An orange No. 21 filter will make a beach seem like a desert.

In contrast to color photography, the subject of a black-and-white photograph is represented by different tones of gray, varying from white to black. In color photographs, each color (or hue) of the spectrum has a number of *tones* relating to the brightness of the color, providing another dimension of separation and definition for any object within the photograph.

Pete Turner

Filters can make a great impact on a photograph, heightening drama by emphasizing graphic aspects. At left, a green filter gives this shadow on a wall an eerie cast, while on page 19, the amber filter emphasizes the urban landscape.

COMPOSING PHOTOGRAPHS

Morton Beebe

When you are composing a color picture, you should ask yourself this very important question: If you remove the color, what do you have? Although many of the principles of composition hold true for both color and black-and-white photos, color contrast is often critical in much of the basis for making a color photograph.

As an experiment, with color film try to make a photograph that has no color, just black-and-white tones. It is likely you will begin to see color where you originally thought there was none, and you will begin to have an appreciation for just how much color exists in everything you see.

A second way to appreciate color in photographic composition is to shoot all your subjects in black-and-white as you shoot them with color film. Compare the color and the black-and-white photographs. Does the composition remain strong in black-and-white? Look at the balance, the dynamics, the lines and the flow throughout the image. If you are making successful color images, they *should* lose some appeal as black-and-white images. If your color photographs exhibit the same strong graphics and interest as black-and-white images, then you are not taking full advantage of color. By paying close attention to color interplay within your subject, you can improve the composition. Color itself can become the subject of the photograph unless you are aware of this interplay.

By converting a color photograph to black-and-white, you can see what an important element of composition color can be.

COMPOSING PHOTOGRAPHS

THE MEANING AND USE OF LINES

Lines are one of the most effective elements for guiding and directing the viewer's eye. They help to define shapes and establish direction, and create tension or balance within an image. Strictly two-dimensional, lines do not have any depth. They do, however, create depth by their relative placement, shape, and length.

An example of depth created by lines might be railroad tracks leading off into the distance. The two lines are parallel. To your eye and the camera lens, however, they seem to converge, creating the perspective of depth within the flat photograph.

Curved lines, such as the bannisters of a formal staircase, slow the viewer's eye along their path. Curved lines reduce the fast, aggressive motion that straight lines suggest; they convey a softer, more sensuous feeling.

A sense of depth is created when parallel lines, such as road lines, converge in the distance.

ELEMENTS OF COMPOSITION

A curved line invites the viewer's eye to move around a photograph, as in this path through a water lily patch.

Lines can also seem static or stationary. For example, a horizon line establishes a base that supports both the subject and the other elements of the photograph. Vertical lines, like those of a building, seem to flow upward, although lines parallel to the sides of the frame, like those of a picket fence, may create a more static appearance in a photograph.

Diagonal lines in a photograph represent motion and very strong direction. They imply the direction the subject will take. Strategically placed, diagonal lines impart a feeling of either instability or impending action, even to non-moving subjects.

Diagonal lines pull the viewer's eye from the edge of the frame toward the subject. By carefully controlling the placement and number of diagonals in a photograph, you can establish a tension between movement and non-movement, creating an exciting image. Lines can be either pure lines, such as electrical power wires against the sky, or implied, such as the boundaries between areas of different tones or colors.

COMPOSING PHOTOGRAPHS

Joe Devenney

Alain Choisnet

In the photograph at the top, parallel streaks of color in the sky, the horizon, and on the water confirm the calm of this landscape, while in the lower photograph, the diagonal lines created by the camera angle give a sense of movement to this image. Note how additional interest was created by *vignetting.*

SHAPE AND FORM

At first glance, the terms shape and form appear to express the same idea about three-dimensional objects. But in photography, they represent very different approaches.

Think of shape as the two-dimensional projection of an object, such as a silhouette of a giraffe at sunset, or the front of a house shot head-on with no other sides showing. To the viewer, the object could be actually flat, with no depth at all. All shapes are two-dimensional, although they usually represent three-dimensional objects. For instance, a cube photographed straight-on appears as a square in the image. To the viewer, however, the "square" may still register a cube or anything with a square edge.

Form is much more complex than shape. It shows volume. In a photograph, it is the difference between light and dark areas that creates the illusion of three dimensions. Form defines the depth, or three-dimensional quality of an object. In black-and-white photography, form is defined by the variation in density between adjacent areas and by areas of extreme brightness that may contain no density at all.

Jake Rajs

The play of light and shadow on the pyramids indicates their volume.

Hank DeLespinasse

While volume must have shape, shape does not need to have volume, as exemplified by this backlit photograph of a cement plant.

PATTERNS AND TEXTURE

Patterns in nature or in man-made objects represent order. Patterns can either be formed by the shape or surface of a subject or they can be caused by the interplay of light and shadow. Often, in black-and-white photography, patterns become merely light and dark shapes, appearing abstract unless other elements are introduced. In color photographs, patterns are more interesting as they can contain variations of brightness and hues.

Photographs of patterns often lack the impact of the original scene. Unless the pattern is unusual, you are merely photographing repetition. It is often helpful to introduce a small element to the pattern to establish its scale.

Direct oblique light—light which strikes the subject from the side—reveals *texture.* An interplay of light and shadow, texture reveals more depth than a straight pattern.

David Brownell

Richard & Mary Magruder

In the photograph at the top, the element of scale adds interest to the pattern of snow and shadow. In the lower photograph, the irregular pattern of the shadows is pleasing to the eye.

COMPOSING PHOTOGRAPHS

Even though it is diffused, the low angle of the light on the man's face emphasizes texture and adds depth.

Larry Dale Gordon

Texture can be very powerful in revealing information about a subject. Think about a man with a very weathered face. If you were to photograph him under soft frontal light, the texture of his skin would be diminished. But if you photograph this same man with direct light striking his face from one side, highlights and shadows will reveal the texture of his skin and add character to the portrait. *Sidelighting,* with the light falling on a subject from either side, creates dramatic shadows across surfaces and reveals much of the subject's three-dimensional nature, through the highlights and shadows caused by surface texture. Composing with sidelighting can be difficult because of the proliferation of light and dark tones that may obscure or reduce visual interest in the subject. In fact, the light alone often becomes the subject of this type of photograph.

Photographing a young child with direct sidelighting would reveal the surface texture of the skin, but as we think of young children as having smooth skin, this would not be appropriate to the subject. Remember that whatever you photograph—a person or an object—the lighting and composition should be appropriate to the subject.

THE PROPERTIES OF LIGHT

There are three fundamental properties of light that are independent of each other: *quality, intensity* (or *quantity*), and *color.*

The *quality* of light refers to the characteristics of either direct or diffused light. *Direct lighting* results from a single-point light source, such as the sun or a single light bulb. It causes brilliant highlights and deep shadows, and makes photographs appear harsh. Too varied a mixture of shadows and highlights will jar the eye and confuse the viewer since the subject seems hidden beneath the pattern of bright and dark areas.

The angle at which the direct light source strikes the subject drastically affects its appearance. Frontlighting (sun behind you as you take a picture) clearly reveals the details and tones of a subject. Because it minimizes shadows, it diminishes form and texture but stresses shape. Subjects appear flat, two-dimensional.

Sidelighting (sun coming from either side of you) emphasizes shadows. Textures and forms leap out. Subjects now have volume and depth. Plowed fields, rocky beaches, peeling paint, and other richly textured scenes spring forth when struck by sidelight. However, direct, unaltered sidelighting generally

Frank Whitney

The strength of color is apparent in the full sun of midday.

COMPOSING PHOTOGRAPHS

demeans faces because it emphasizes cosmetic flaws and creates deep shadows that hide round cheeks and dimples. But by using a white cardboard reflector or a flash unit to lighten those shadows, you can convert sidelighting into a useful tool to make flattering portraits.

Direct backlighting (when you point the camera towards the light) allows you to create many variations from the conventional, clearly revealed frontlighted scene. Easy to make are silhouettes. To make the subject appear black against a bright background, simply set the exposure for the background and take the picture. When flowers, umbrellas, hair, and other translucent things are backlighted, they seem to glow. Pictures made with backlighting are often very graphic and may have a great sense of depth. Instead of disorganizing the scene, the harsh shadows and bright highlights of backlighting almost always enliven it. The disadvantage of backlighting is that the range of brightness from dark to light is so wide that film cannot reproduce detail in both highlights and shadows. You must choose which area to show detail or use a flash to lighten the shadows.

André Gallant

Bright colors add interest to this diffused-light portrait.

ELEMENTS OF COMPOSITION

The midday hours may be described as the most common form of direct lighting. The near-overhead position of the sun causes toplighting. Shadows shrink and fall in awkward positions, such as under the eyes and nose. Most subjects do not thrive under toplighting, making midday a difficult time to compose attractive photographs.

Diffused lighting is very soft and lacks the extreme contrasts of direct light. It is exemplified by the light on a cloudy but bright day; tones are muted, and shadows are soft and ill-defined. It is excellent for people, as it minimizes skin flaws and flatters faces. Diffused light also reveals subtler variations in hues than direct light, and leaves a gentler, more passive impression. Use it to show the many hues in a flower garden or the rich greens of mountain forests. To avoid the bald and boring gray sky, simply exclude it by tilting your camera down.

John P. Kelly

Sidelighting, as in this photograph, emphasizes depth relationships.

COMPOSING PHOTOGRAPHS

Photographs taken indoors with daylight film and tungsten bulbs can appear orangish because of the film's color balance.

Bill Varie

Intensity, the second property of light, is a measurable quantity, and relates to the brightness of incidental light within a scene. It affects the tonal range and brilliance of the recorded tones.

The *color* of light varies with the type of light source and the surroundings of the subject and, in the case of daylight, the time of day. Unlike the color of the subject itself, the color of daylight relates directly to the time of day and carries the moods associated with those times. The blues of twilight tranquilize and soothe as they represent awaking or settling down. The reds and oranges of a low sun just appearing or disappearing seem poignant and fleeting as they indicate our reliance on the sun. The bold neutral light of midday animates and invigorates—it represents the time we are most active—working, playing, shopping, but certainly not sleeping.

ELEMENTS OF COMPOSITION

PART TWO

CAMERA TECHNIQUES FOR CONTROLLING COMPOSITION

Chris Alan Wilton

Over the past decade 35 mm cameras have become increasingly automatic, so you often do not need to set any controls at all. Several manual controls have either disappeared entirely or now work automatically. However, such automation is not always to your benefit since some controls affect a photo's appearance. Two functions you can still control in many SLR cameras are *shutter speed* and *lens opening,* commonly called *aperture.* These two functions not only control the exposure of film but can dramatically affect image sharpness.

Automatic SLR cameras use up to four types of exposure control, and most cameras have at least two ways to control exposure. With the first, called *aperture-priority,* you select a lens opening and the camera then selects a shutter speed for proper exposure. With the second type, called *shutter-priority,* you set the shutter speed and the camera sets the aperture. With the third type, called *program mode,* you do nothing—a computer in the camera sets the aperture and shutter speed to give correct exposure. Common to SLR cameras and often the only mode in point-and-shoot cameras, the program mode prevents you from controlling what the camera is doing. Many SLR cameras offer several program modes that allow you to indirectly alter shutter speed and aperture. For example, the depth program sets a small aperture for great depth of field (front-to-back scene sharpness); the action program sets a fast shutter speed to show moving subjects sharply. And some cameras have a *manual mode* that requires you to set both the shutter speed and the aperture. Program modes are essential for action and other spontaneous photography. But for still-life, portrait and landscape photography, you can work more methodically if you use the camera in the manual or aperture-priority mode.

In Part Two, we will discuss how a camera sees, how to reveal depth through lighting and perspective, as well as how lens focal length affects composition. We will also show you how to use the photographic frame to its best advantage, how to manipulate with selective focus to emphasize the subject, how to choose shutter speed, and how to set the proper exposure and film.

HOW A CAMERA SEES

The view provided by the two forward-looking eyes of humans is called binocular vision. Since your eyes are set a few inches apart, each sees a slightly different view—a very valuable feature that enables you to better perceive depth.

A camera, however, uses only one eye, the lens, to record a scene. Furthermore, the scene it records is revealed on a flat piece of paper. How then can a flat piece of paper drawn on by a one-eyed lens reveal the depth you saw when viewing Yosemite's Half Dome from Glacier Point or even the short depth of your backyard? The answer is through careful use of lighting and perspective, techniques long used by artists.

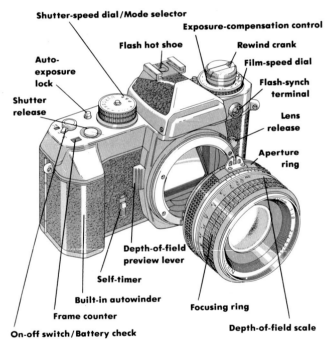

Shutter-speed dial/Mode selector

Exposure-compensation control

Flash hot shoe

Rewind crank

Auto-exposure lock

Film-speed dial

Flash-synch terminal

Shutter release

Lens release

Aperture ring

Depth-of-field preview lever

Self-timer

Built-in autowinder

Focusing ring

Frame counter

Depth-of-field scale

On-off switch/Battery check

Some cameras have many controls for manually adjusting the film speed setting, aperture, and shutter speed.

COMPOSING PHOTOGRAPHS

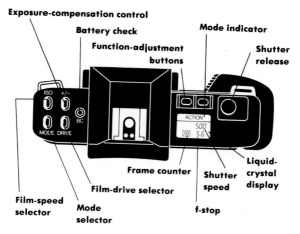

Exposure-compensation control
Battery check
Mode indicator
Function-adjustment buttons
Shutter release

ISO +/−
BC
MODE DRIVE
ACTION
500
10 5.6

Frame counter
Shutter speed
Liquid-crystal display
Film-drive selector
Film-speed selector
Mode selector
f-stop

SHOWING DEPTH

Although a photograph is a two-dimensional object, its success as a composition often relies on how effectively it renders a three-dimensional scene.

Through lighting and perspective, you can realistically show a scene's three dimensions.

Lighting. If you were to make a close-up photo of a ping-pong ball outdoors on a cloudy day (flat lighting), it would appear as a circle in the picture. Any viewer other than yourself would be hard-pressed to say whether it was a ping-pong ball, a disk of wood, or the end of a cylinder. However, if the sun were to come out in the early morning or late afternoon and you positioned yourself so the sun was at your side, you could produce a picture that would clearly depict the ping-pong ball as a sphere. Such sidelighting creates a strong shadow on one side of the subject that reveals its volume. (You have just learned the artist's trick of using shading to reveal form.)

Sidelighting invariably conveys depth in both overall scenes and individual subjects. Sidelighting on a face creates nose, cheek, and lip shadows that define the contours of the face. Such lighting may not flatter a face but it does show its three dimensions.

In larger scenes, backlighting excels in conveying depth by directing long shadows toward the camera. Shadows extending from the subject toward the camera may even exaggerate the depth of a scene.

Perspective. You can also stress the depth of a scene by composing it to reveal the linear perspective inherent in the scene. Linear perspective is the seeming convergence of parallel lines. Stand at the base of a skyscraper and peer toward its top. The sides of the building seem to converge, though you know they don't. Buildings, roads, fences, beaches, fields—all include lines that convey linear perspective. To emphasize linear perspective, position yourself at the angle that best shows parallel lines in the scene converging. To stress depth in a building, don't face it head-on; instead, stand to one side so its lines seem to run obliquely through the picture.

You can also reveal depth by including subjects in both the immediate foreground and background. For instance, if you are photographing a lighthouse at the end of a rocky peninsula, don't frame the scene so only the distant lighthouse shows. Instead, stoop down and include some nearby rocks and the lighthouse. Although in the picture the rocks may appear bigger than the lighthouse, the mind readily converts this size differ-

COMPOSING PHOTOGRAPHS

Great depth of field can also indicate distance, as in this photograph. On page 36, the contrast of bright subjects against a dark background conveys a sense of depth.

ence into a measure of distance. It sees depth, not size difference. If you include a foreground subject, set a small aperture, such as *f*/11, so both foreground and background appear sharp in the picture.

LENS FOCAL LENGTH AND COMPOSITION

The focal length of a lens often determines how you compose a scene, and the greatest advantage of the SLR camera is that you can use lenses of different focal lengths. Lenses for SLR cameras are classified according to their focal length as normal, wide-angle, or telephoto.

The normal lens is approximately 50 mm in focal length. Although a normal lens only provides a natural rendition of distance relationships in a scene, you can use it creatively to control other aspects of composition. The normal lens has some of the capabilities of both wide-angle and telephoto lenses. Because a normal lens has a large maximum aperture, you can use it for *selective focus* (subject in focus, background very out of focus) similar to that obtained with a telephoto lens. At small apertures around *f*/11 or *f*/16, it can provide the great depth of field usually associated with wide-angle lenses.

CAMERA TECHNIQUES

With wide-angle lenses you can create stunningly deep perspective in a photograph, emphasizing the distance between foreground objects and the background. Also, from a given

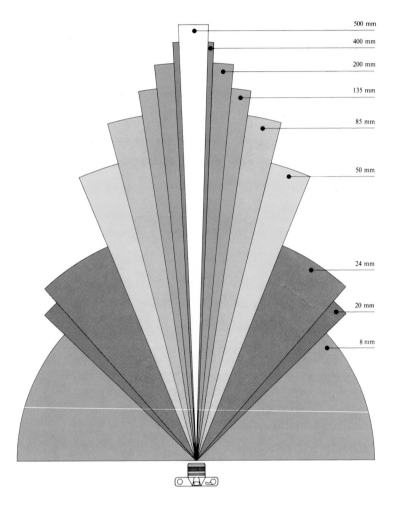

500 mm
400 mm
200 mm
135 mm
85 mm
50 mm
24 mm
20 mm
8 mm

A wide-angle lens is only one of various focal lengths shown on this diagram.

A wide-angle lens can give you great depth of field, keeping everything in focus.

distance, wide-angle lenses keep more of the scene in sharp focus than normal or telephoto lenses do. Because you have to get so close to the subject to make it big, wide-angle lenses are much harder to use for selective focus.

For a 35 mm camera, a wide-angle lens is any lens having a focal length less than 45 mm. In general, a wide-angle lens allows you to include a broader area from a specific distance than a normal lens does. It accomplishes this by reducing the image size.

Telephoto lenses have focal lengths greater than 60 mm. They magnify the subject and the background, bringing them closer to you in the viewfinder. These lenses seemingly compress distance between objects at different distances from the camera, making them appear to be stacked together. At close distances, telephoto lenses give you very shallow depth of field at most aperture settings. This lets you isolate a subject by making the background and foreground appear out of focus, with just the main subject sharp. Short telephoto focal-length lenses (80 to 105 mm) provide very natural-looking perspective, and closely approximate what your eyes would see. For this reason, they are a natural choice for portraits. For subduing a distracting background or creating a compressed perspective, the telephoto lens has no equal.

Ira Block

John P. Kelly

Telephoto lenses give short depth of field, and are excellent for getting close-up shots of dangerous animals or exciting action.

THE PHOTOGRAPHIC FRAME

The edges of the camera viewfinder form a frame that isolates your subject from its surroundings; its proportions depend on the type of camera. In all current "full-frame" 35 mm cameras, the sides of the viewfinder have a ratio of 3 to 2. The long side of the frame is 1 1/2 times the short side. This frame proportion defines how you view the world in your photos.

You can use the photographic frame to its best advantage by making it an active part of your composition. To do this, you must understand what it means to "fill" the frame, and what horizontal or vertical framing, as well as the use of secondary frames, can mean to your composition.

Luis Castañeda

When you hold an SLR camera as close to your eye as possible, you can compose your photographs right up to the edge of the viewfinder.

Moving closer, whether physically or by using a tele-photo lens, can help your composition immensely.

COMPOSING PHOTOGRAPHS

Filling the frame. One problem that even experienced photographers encounter when looking into the viewfinder is mind over matter.

What does this mean? Have you ever reviewed what you thought would be a great shot of your dog resting in a field and discovered that the photo shows a lot of field and very little dog? But you were sure the viewfinder was absolutely filled with the dog!

This happens because your mind concentrates on the dog. It fills your mental image but not the photographic frame. When composing an image, scan the viewfinder to see how much empty space it includes. Chances are you'll want to move closer to your subject. When the subject fills the picture, you've made it clear what the subject is and you've shown its many details and nuances. You will see a difference in your photos almost immediately.

Harold Sund

Horizontal framing gives a feeling of calm and stability, as in this atmospheric seascape.

Horizontal vs. vertical framing. In 35 mm cameras, the shape of the frame lets you make either horizontal or vertical pictures. A horizontal format implies motion or direction across a broad expanse. It also limits the amount of vertical vision and foreground within the frame. Its implied low center of gravity makes it seem more stable than the vertical format. A vertical format implies vertical motion, height, and upward direction. When you use a vertical composition with wide-angle lenses, the foreground becomes very important, because these lenses emphasize perspective, expanding the apparent distance by altering the relationship between the foreground and background.

One of the most common errors in composition is making a horizontal portrait with a person in the center of the frame. Such a portrait usually leaves some space above the person's head and often places the face and eyes at the exact center of the frame. Always consider whether a vertical format might be more effective than a horizontal one.

TIPS FOR MAKING VERTICAL PHOTOGRAPHS

- Practice holding your camera vertically more often; visualize each subject as if you were shooting a magazine cover.
- Determine if there are more vertical lines than horizontal ones.
- Remember what you are attempting to show in your picture.
- Horizontal photographs tend to show a broad expanse; vertical pictures are more specific and limit the tendency of your eyes to wander from side to side.

Secondary frames. Making a photograph automatically places a frame around the subject. The photographic frame isolates and separates the subject from its environment and draws the attention of the viewer to the subject.

COMPOSING PHOTOGRAPHS

In this comparison, the vertical photograph emphasizes the distance of the barn from the foreground, while in the photograph below, the horizontal aspects of the building are emphasized.

Robert Herko

Robert Herko

You can further isolate and concentrate attention on your subject by using a picture element to create a second frame in your photograph. A second frame creates a greater sense of depth and can eliminate distracting objects around your subject. Doorways, arching tree branches, and the rails of a fence are a few common sources to serve as frames.

Tim Bieber, Inc.

Eric L. Wheater

In the top photograph, the bright window frame adds appeal to this pastel portrait, and concentrates attention on the cat. In the lower photograph, an interesting combination of color and curves frames the children in the red tube.

COMPOSING PHOTOGRAPHS

DEPTH OF FIELD AND SELECTIVE FOCUS

Although shutter speed and aperture work together to control how much light exposes the film, they affect the appearance of the image very differently. Shutter speed affects only moving subjects. *Lens aperture affects all subjects.*

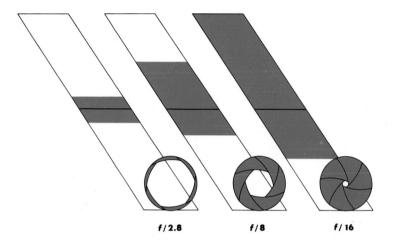

f / 2.8   f / 8   f / 16

How sharp and wide your depth of field is depends on the aperture at which your camera is set. The wider the aperture, the shallower the depth of field.

Lens aperture determines the range of focus in the image. In general, if you would like everything from foreground to background to be in focus, you would use a very small aperture, indicated by one of the higher *f*-numbers such as *f*/11. If you want only a specific part of a scene to be in sharp focus, you'd use a wider aperture, such as *f*/2.8 and position your subject near the camera to separate it from the background. This technique, called *selective focus,* makes your subject stand out from the background. By using this technique, you can make the background very blurred (out-of-focus), while your subject is sharp. This is useful when background clutter distracts the eye from the main subject.

When you are using a non-SLR camera, you can't see the scene as the lens "sees" it because the viewfinder is separate from the lens. But with an SLR camera, you view the scene right through the lens. However, when you are viewing the scene, the camera lens is always set to the largest aperture to provide a bright image in the viewfinder for focusing. If the lens is set at any aperture other than its largest *f*-number, you are not seeing the scene as the lens will when you trip the shutter.

To see just what will be in focus, press the *depth-of-field preview button* (if your camera has one) to set the lens to the aperture that the camera will use to expose the film. The viewfinder will darken when you use the depth-of-field preview but, with a little experience, you will be able to judge how the scene will look. You can also use the depth-of-field scale on your lens that will be used during picture-taking to determine the range of sharpness for the aperture you've chosen. Your camera manual should explain how to use this scale for your camera.

With selective focus, you make the background completely out of focus to become an abstract backdrop for a portrait.

Melchior DiGiacomo

COMPOSING PHOTOGRAPHS

Selective focus can be used to diminish a cluttered background.

Foustino

SHUTTER SPEED

You can use shutter speed—the time the shutter is open to expose the film—to produce effects very different from those controlled by lens aperture. If your camera is stationary, and your subject is not moving, the effect of shutter speed is not really noticeable. But if the camera is stationary and the subject is moving, different shutter speeds will create very different results. Long shutter speeds will blur moving subjects; short ones will show them sharp.

With blur, you can convey the impression of motion in a still image. The amount of blur you show communicates the relative speed of the subject.

Hans Wolf

Robert Herko

Using a slow shutter speed will blur movement, as in the flowing river at the top, or the auto race in the lower photograph.

COMPOSING PHOTOGRAPHS

Short exposure times such as 1/1000 second will stop almost any moving subject and record a virtually motionless image on film. But combinations of slower shutter speeds and different types of motion will create varying degrees of blur, ranging from slight to total streaking. It's even possible to keep the shutter open so long that a subject moving through the field of view will not be recorded at all. This happens when you use a very long exposure (several seconds to several minutes) and the subject doesn't remain in the scene long enough for light reflecting from it to be recorded on the film. This is one way to remove traffic and people from crowded outdoor scenes; only people or cars that are stationary for a long enough period will be visible in the photograph. To obtain slow shutter speeds, use a low-speed film such as KODAK EKTAR 25 Film and shoot on a cloudy day at a small aperture.

With a moving subject, you can also create blur by taking the picture as you move the camera to track the subject; try to keep the subject in the same spot in the viewfinder as you move the camera. The subject will appear fairly sharp, but the background will be blurred (see photograph on page 57). This is called panning the camera. When you pan the camera, use a moderate shutter speed, ranging from 1/30 to 1/125 second—or experiment with a slower shutter speed, such as 1/8 second but take lots of photos since the results will be unpredictable. Be sure to keep moving the camera as you press the shutter release and to "follow through" as you would with a tennis or golf swing.

Although you can move the camera to blur a still subject, the results typically look like a mistake (you had the jitters) or puzzling. However, in the name of creativity, you should be willing to try anything.

By freezing the movement of a subject in a photo, you can create a very different impression from that yielded by blur. Blur emphasizes motion. A sharp image of a subject stresses strength, agility, balance. Timing and viewpoint are crucial. Use a low viewpoint to reinforce a subject's strength. Make the viewer feel he is about to be trampled by a running back or leaped over by a hurdler. Use an eye-level view to reveal grace. Choose the viewpoint that best reveals the subject's posture in action. Usually this won't be head-on but from an oblique angle that clearly reveals legs galloping or arms stretching to make a catch. Take the picture just before you expect the climactic moment to occur. If you wait until that moment, the delay in your reaction may cause you to miss it. If you know the action is going to occur in a particular spot, you may want to prefocus on that spot, even if you're using an autofocus camera. To stop action, use a fast shutter speed, such as 1/1000 second, and a high-speed film, such as KODACOLOR GOLD 400 Film.

Leo Mason

Fast shutter speeds can freeze motion, as in the photo of the high jumper at top, and the surfer below.

Don King

EXPOSURE

Although accurate exposure may not be critical with negative films, it is with slide films. Using color-slide film is the best way to learn proper exposure techniques. Color-slide film requires accurate exposure, because there is no interim printing step and no room for compensation.

With slide film, variations in exposure can create dramatic effects that make exposure a creative control. Slight overexposure, about 1/2 to 1 full stop, will lighten a scene. Colors will become more pastel, and will convey a sense of "airy," open space. With an appropriate subject, this lightening can evoke a sense of happiness and freshness. With the proper subject matter, slight underexposure, 1/2 to 1 full stop, will create a dark and brooding sense of gloom, or heaviness. Colors will be more saturated and intense. Even light tones such as yellow and orange become visually heavy.

Sigi Bunn

Intentional overexposure can convey a feeling of airiness.

The next time you photograph a clear sunset, try *bracketing* your exposure by taking additional photos giving one stop over and one under the indicated exposure. If you use color-slide film, the images will range from a light and happy image to an intense, saturated deep image that expresses the sadness of the end of another day. None of the exposures is "better" than another, because the primary purpose of your photograph is to communicate how you feel.

Gerald Brimacombe

The Image Bank

Intentional underexposure in the photo at top has created a dramatic silhouette, while intentional overexposure and diffusion created by the snowstorm give an impressionistic look to an overcast day.

COMPOSING PHOTOGRAPHS

FILM

An obvious fact in choosing a film is matching film speed to the lighting conditions you'll be shooting in. For bright days, you'd normally choose a low- or medium-speed film. For cloudy days (or dimly lighted scenes), you would normally pick a high-speed film.

But film has other traits that subtly influence your compositions. Color saturation, sharpness, and graininess (the inherent texture of a film) depend partly on film speed. Low- and medium-speed films, such as KODAK EKTAR 25 and 125 and KODACOLOR GOLD 100, have richer, brighter colors than higher-speed films. The differences in color saturation may not be obvious even in side-by-side comparisons, but they are there.

The better sharpness and finer grain of lower-speed films may be even more important. EKTAR 25 and 125 Films are the finest-grained color-negative films in their respective speed classes. For

When detail and rich color are crucial to a photograph, use a low- or medium-speed film, such as KODAK EKTAR 125 Film.

Steve Kelly / Courtesy of Eastman Kodak Co.

B. Banks/Courtesy of Eastman Kodak Co.

Using a black-and-white film (here KODAK T-MAX 400 Professional Film) will help reinforce a mood, such as the one created by the dog's baleful expression.

the best reproduction of still-lifes and landscapes rich with detail, you should use such fine-grained films. Fine grain is also important in landscapes dominated by sky or water. The uniform midtones of sky and water readily reveal a graininess that may detract from the scene.

Extremely fine grain does not enhance all compositions. For existing-light and action scenes, you may have no choice but to use a high-speed film with more apparent grain. But increased graininess actually makes such scenes look more realistic. Because newspaper and magazine photographs of current events have traditionally been grainy, we have been conditioned to associate graininess with realism. Actually the great improvements in films have so minimized grain that it's no longer easy

COMPOSING PHOTOGRAPHS

to show. With KODACOLOR GOLD 400 Film, graininess will be gently revealed. It becomes more apparent in the very-high speed KODACOLOR GOLD 1600 Film.

The long tradition of black-and-white film in photojournalism and fine-art photography makes black-and-white film an appropriate choice for many compositions. If you don't lean toward either of those categories, then simply use black-and-white film when a subject's composition is attractive but its colors aren't. KODAK T-MAX 100 and 400 Professional Films both give exceptional results.

Derek Doeffinger/Courtesy of Eastman Kodak Co.

KODACOLOR GOLD 100 or 200 Film works well when you want to pan with a moving subject to convey action.

PUTTING IT ALL TOGETHER

Having practiced camera handling until adjusting focus and setting exposure become second nature; having experimented with and varied your subject placement by employing the rule of thirds; having learned the importance of each nuance of color, light and line, as well as how to use them to bring a sense of three-dimensionality to your photographs, you might ask: What's left? If you are still not happy with your pictures, perhaps it's because you still need to bring everything you've learned together.

Good composition will not simply happen. You, the photographer, must organize the raw material you find into a cohesive image. And this means you must integrate what you have learned about composition thus far.

Review the photographs you have taken before and after reading the previous sections of this book. Can you see a difference? If you can, but are still not satisfied with your photographs, perhaps it is because they are still missing that elusive quality—your personal style—that only you can give them.

How does one go about interjecting one's distinct personality into one's photographs? What is style, and can the amateur photographer ever hope to possess as much of it as the professional?

The elements of composition, camera techniques, and exposure control are like the ingredients of a good recipe. One without the rest cannot make a complete photograph or tell the complete story. But once you have learned these things and know how and when to apply them, then you combine elements to form a new language, or *visual expression,* that has understanding and appeal, not only for your immediate audience, but for the world at large.

In Part Three, we examine the effects your point of view, the horizon, negative space, and subject dominance have on your composition, and how you can use images to convey abstractions and themes, as well as balance, direction, and tension. We'll also show you how to improve composition by interjecting your personality into your photos.

Benn Mitchell

Photographing children from slightly below the adult eye level emphasizes their diminutive charm without distortion.

POINT OF VIEW

One of the best ways to break the cliche of making photographs at your own eye level is to ask yourself these questions:

DO YOU...

- take most photographs while standing upright?
- feel there is an unwritten law that says every photograph should be taken at your eye level?
- wonder what your pet sees at its eye level?
- ever wonder just how tall and imposing you must be to children?

A common disappointment to parents is the photograph made of their small child from an adult's standing height. It probably shows the top of the child's head, or the child's face straining to look up at you and smile. Why not get down to the level that shows the subject properly? When you photograph children, get right down to their level; try to show them as other children see them. Try what most professional photographers do when they photograph people: position the lens at or near the level of the subject's waist to achieve a balanced perspective.

By lowering your viewpoint, you can reveal a different perspective, whether the subject is a child, another adult, or a flower in a field. The lower viewing angle will promote your subject and provide more emphasis than an overhead view. By shooting from a lower angle, you impart greater size and scale to your subject.

Tim Bieber, Inc.

Portraits of children are usually best when taken at eye level.

THE HORIZON

The placement of the horizon in a scenic photograph often determines the character of the photo. Dividing the frame into two equal segments by placing the horizon in the center produces a static, indecisive rendition. Neither the sky nor the ground will command attention. The viewer's eye will wander back and forth between the two areas instead of being drawn to the subject.

Placing the horizon low in the frame instills a sense of spaciousness, of freedom and a lack of earthly ties. The sky draws the viewer's attention. This approach works well when you want to convey a sense of awe or dwarf an earthbound subject. A high horizon line brings attention to the ground and minimizes the impact of sky. It draws attention to foreground objects and shows textures in the landscape.

Luis Castañeda

Centering the horizon gives a static appearance to the image.

COMPOSING PHOTOGRAPHS

Albert Normandin

Grant V. Faint

A low horizon, as in the photo at top, gives a feeling of breadth and wide open spaces to a landscape, while the high horizon in the lower photo emphasizes distance and the physical difficulty of the terrain.

NEGATIVE SPACE

"Negative space" describes the space between objects in a photograph. Negative space sometimes commands attention because of its shape and often competes for attention with the subject. A viewer may perceive the different shape of the space as an object. When that happens, the space actually functions as a secondary subject.

Areas of negative space within a photograph may disrupt composition. In photographs of patterns, the negative spaces may form a pattern that predominates. Large dark areas of negative space can also block visual flow and balance.

On the other hand, negative space can help define your subject. A dark silhouette of a couple may look like an indistinguishable blob unless you separate them with negative space.

Constant practice at visualizing the shapes within a scene will help you find and evaluate negative space before you take the picture. One trick that helps is to squint slightly as you look at the scene through the viewfinder so that the image is reduced in brightness and definition. This will help you to envision the scene as areas of light and dark shapes rather than the three-dimensional objects that are actually present.

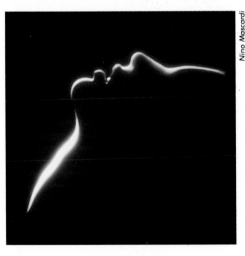

Negative space fills in the form of this rimlighted subject.

Nino Mascardi

In the photograph at the right, negative space delineates this silhouette of Jefferson, while below, the patterns caused by shadows animate this image.

PUTTING IT ALL TOGETHER

SUBJECT DOMINANCE

Quite often the subject of a photograph is lost in its environment—in the background, in the foreground, or among other objects in the frame. You can emphasize the main subject and subordinate the secondary elements in several ways.

If you want your subject to jump out from the background, try one of these techniques:

TO SEPARATE YOUR SUBJECT FROM THE BACKGROUND

- Place the main subject at one of the points suggested by the "rule of thirds" (see page 14). These points command the viewer's attention and allow you to establish a dynamic perspective against the background.
- Place the subject at the center of the frame and move closer. Make the image of the subject large enough to draw attention to the centralized placement.
- Simply make the subject large in relation to the rest of the scene. Use a wide-angle lens to emphasize the subject in the foreground while reducing the size of any objects in the background. Although the scale will be distorted, this is a powerful technique for creating a sense of depth.
- Use color to create attention points. Any small area of contrasting color placed within a larger area will draw the viewer's attention.
- Use *selective focus* (see pages 47–49) to isolate your subject from the background. Move near to the subject and set a large aperture on a normal or telephoto lens to blur the background.

The one situation in which your subject should not command the greatest attention is when you want your subject to be part of a larger environment. For example, if you want to

In the photograph at the right, the subjects are part of the overall composition. Below, the subject's dominance is enhanced by his red outfit.

John B. Kelly

Patti McConville

In this portrait, the centered subject dominates the picture entirely.

show the extent of a dairy farm, it's important to show some cows in a field. But the cows do not have to be very large to show that the field is a dairy pasture. If your subject supports a larger theme, balance the size of the elements so that they support the theme.

ABSTRACTION AND THEME

Has a photograph or piece of art ever triggered a memory or recalled a mood, a place, or a time? Why is it that some images evoke memories and others do not?

It's because certain shapes, colors, and lines are evocative. They stand for specific thoughts, themes, and emotions. Warm tones, such as bright orange and red mean action, strength, and movement; blue or cooler tones evoke thoughts of tranquility,

COMPOSING PHOTOGRAPHS

calm, stability—often mystery. Misty reddish tones do not evoke the same mood as misty blues, so color has a fundamental impact on how we react to an image.

Lines and shapes also add to the feeling in a photograph. Their direction and placement establishes dynamic or passive moods.

Theme is the key to arranging all the elements at your disposal to make a clear presentation to the viewer. Your approach must be appropriate to your subject matter. For example, you wouldn't show a theme of aggression with soft, diffused lighting and primarily pastel tones. For most people, aggression is far better symbolized by hard light, strong colors and a sense of motion. It is therefore essential to learn the *visual language of emotion.*

When you want to express a particular theme, try to remove all objects and details that don't contribute to the message. Simplicity and unity are the key to creating captivating images.

Michael Melford

This photograph of gears illustrates the beauty of technology.

James H. Carmichael, Jr.

This close-up of a birdwing butterfly shows the theme of adaptation.

When you can abstract the essential elements of your subject and effectively present your theme, you will be an effective communicator.

Think of a specific theme, such as strength. How can you say "strength" in the simplest terms? You could show a gym filled with exercise machines and weights, but what would this really say about strength? Why not go farther and show a very muscular arm, tensed as it lifts a weight? By using directional sidelighting, you can emphasize the veins and bulging muscles. Using a wide-angle lens very close to the arm would further emphasize the bulge of the muscles, expanding the perspective and placing more emphasis on the size of the muscles. In selecting the essentials of a theme, consider the image as a compositional whole, made up not only of the placement of the subject in the viewfinder, but of the lighting, the color, the implied dynamics, and perspective.

Don't remove so much detail that the theme will be lost to the viewer. If your photograph requires verbal explanation or justification, you've removed too much information. Effective abstracting should present enough detail to communicate the theme, but leave room for personal interpretation by the viewer.

COMPOSING PHOTOGRAPHS

BALANCE, DIRECTION, AND TENSION

Good photographs have visual balance, a harmonic configuring of light and dark tones, of large and small shapes, of straight and curved lines, of smooth and rough textures, of loud and quiet colors. They also have focal points on which the viewer's eye can rest.

You can produce two types of balance in a photograph: *static balance,* where the lack of tension and competition between the tones, shapes and colors arrests the viewer's attention; and *dynamic balance,* in which controlled tension moves the viewer's eye to specific points. Dynamic balance is much harder to achieve because the shapes, colors, and tones compete with each other, as well as with the expectations of the viewer.

To understand balance, you must understand the nature of tones and colors. Humans perceive dark tones as heavier than light tones. This is also true with colors. We perceive blue as heavier than yellow, red as heavier than pink. Darker tones of the same hue also carry more weight than lighter tones.

Other factors that contribute to balance are light and shadow, and dynamics implied by lines of motion or curves that the eye tends to follow. Providing equivalent weight on opposite sides of a photograph means the viewer won't see the picture

Al Satterwhite

Here, the opposing directions of the subject and his shadow create a dynamic balance.

David Brownell

In the top photograph, the uniform tones and lines of the bridge create a static balance. Equally effective is the dynamic balance in the lower photograph, accomplished by the many diagonals of the bridge flowing to the right being offset by the small boat moving to the left.

Eric Schweikardt

COMPOSING PHOTOGRAPHS

as falling out of the frame or tipping over on itself. However, if you want to remove equivalent weight to express an idea of imbalance, then by all means, try it and see if it works!

While horizontal lines express stability and calm, vertical lines maintain a precarious balance; diagonal lines, on the other hand, are unstable and full of motion. Experience with gravity makes us see diagonal lines as falling, or in a temporary state that demands resolution. Used strategically, diagonal lines can invigorate images. Their overuse in pictures will jar and repulse the viewer.

When a photograph is made moments—or even a split second—before an action commences, the implied action creates tension. Think about runners poised at the starting line of a race. A photograph taken an instant before the starter's gun fires will show the tension in each of the runners and imply their motion down the track an instant later.

Another way to generate tension within a photograph is through use of *implied lines.* Much more subtle in application than explicit lines, implied lines result from the relationship between shapes (think of constellations), negative spaces and contrasts within the image.

CHANGING THE RULES

As a photographer, you should learn all the "rules," but know when to break them.

Solidify your ideas and emotions in pictures by exploring your subject and employing good composition. Consider the guidelines we've discussed. But once you've considered them feel free to ignore them anytime you think you've found a better way of constructing your photograph. Depart from the crowds who stand at one spot taking pictures of the Statue of Liberty; find another view that shows the grandeur you feel. Taking pictures should make you feel good; and as you view them in the coming years, they should help you and others to recall the emotions and experiences of the time.

Vary your approach. There is no right way to photograph a subject. Choice of film, lighting, and lenses is as individual as the person making the photograph. The way you feel at the particular moment greatly influences how you portray your subject. Quite often, a professional photographer will return to the same location many times, in many seasons, or even at different times of the day; none of the photographs he makes will be exactly the same. Subtle differences in framing, subject position, lighting, weather and the mood of the photographer affect the image.

Jeff Smith

Look around; use your imagination to come up with different angles.

COMPOSING PHOTOGRAPHS

Being able to capture the moment is a key aspect of personal style.

Elyse Lewin

PERSONAL STYLE

You can immediately recognize the photographs of many professional photographers by their style. Although subject matter and composition may vary widely, the style of the photographs stands out like a signature.

You reveal a part of your personality each time you make a photograph. The very subject you choose reflects your interests, as does the composition. The composition is made from what you see, and its unifying elements are content and style. Although they are not separate elements, they determine the ultimate appearance of a photo.

Content in a photo consists of two basic parts: the subject, which is the center of interest and commands the most attention, and the background (sometimes called just "ground"), which may both support and further define the subject. When you compose a photograph, you arrange these two parts to emphasize your intentions.

Be it a busy thoroughfare, a quiet moment by the lake, or a woman walking in a snowstorm (as on page 77), your approach to the subject will determine whether you capture a memorable image.

Chris Hackett

Style is how you manipulate the content with lighting, perspective, placement, timing, and other factors. Style expresses your response to and interpretation of the content. Although style extends to the subjects selected, it is easier to think of it as the ways you use to show the subject.

Your photographic style will depend on your personality. It can be flamboyant, soft-spoken, subtle, sarcastic, loud, bold, sophisticated. You must ask yourself what really matters to you, and find a way to express that on film.

CONCLUSION. Using the tips and techniques found in *Composing Photographs,* you will begin to see art forming in your photography. You may detect it in subject position, the type of light you like, the subject matter, or a theme common to your images.

Experiment! Find the combination of film, camera, lens, etc., that you feel comfortable with and that gives you pleasing results. Try new viewpoints, subject matter, and lighting. Work with the language of photography to broaden your expressive vocabulary. Don't be afraid to fail. It's through these failures that you learn what will work for you.

GLOSSARY OF TERMS

Angle of view—The extent of the area "seen" by a lens. A wide-angle lens includes more of a scene than does a normal or tele-photo lens.

Aperture—Lens opening. The opening in a lens system through which light passes. The size is either fixed or adjustable. Lens openings are expressed as *f*-numbers.

Aperture-priority—A form of exposure control in which you select the aperture and the camera adjusts the shutter speed for correct exposure.

Autofocus—Used to describe cameras that focus automatically on the subject when you aim the camera so that the subject is within the autofocus marks or brackets in the viewfinder.

Automatic flash—A system that uses an electronic light sensor that is designed to produce proper flash exposures.

Backlighting—Light shining on the subject from the direction opposite the camera.

Balance—Placement of colors, light and dark masses, or large and small objects in a picture to create harmony and equilibrium. In dynamic balance, tension moves the viewer's eye to specific points; in static balance, the lack of tension captures attention.

Bounce flash—A technique in which flash is directed at (or "bounced" off) a large reflective surface to provide softer, more diffused illumination.

Bracketing—Making extra photographs at exposure settings to provide more and less exposure than the calculated or recommended setting—for example, at +1, +2, −1, and −2 stops from the calculated setting.

Built-in flash unit—A non-detachable unit that is a part of the camera. It is usually turned on by a button, but some units will automatically activate when the meter determines that the scene is too dark for proper exposure without flash.

Color compensating (CC) filter—A filter used to produce relatively small alterations in the color balance of a photograph to compensate for the color bias of a light source on the film itself.

Color temperature—A measurement of the color quality of light sources; expressed in degrees Kelvin (K).

Color of light—See "Color temperature."

Conversion filter—A filter used to balance film to a light source different from the source for which it is designed.

Daylight-balanced film—Film balanced to produce accurate color rendition in daylight or with electronic flash.

Depth of field—The distance between the nearest and farthest objects in a scene that appear in acceptable focus in a photograph.

Depth-of-field preview button—A camera control that allows you to see the depth of field in the scene before you take the picture.

Diffusion—Softening of detail in a photograph by using a diffusion filter or other material that scatters light.

Diffusion filter—A type of filter that diffuses light. Diffusion filters come in varying strengths: No.1 is the weakest; mist and fog filters are considerably stronger.

Direct flash—Flash that strikes the subject directly.

Direct lighting—Light that strikes the subject directly.

Electronic flash—A brief but intense burst of light from the flashtube of a built-in or detachable flash unit; used to supplement existing light or provide the main light on the subject.

Exposure—The amount of light that acts on a photographic material; a product of the intensity (controlled by the lens opening) and the duration (controlled by the shutter speed) of light striking the film.

Exposure meter—An instrument—either built into a camera or a separate, hand-held unit—that measures the intensity of light; used to determine the aperture and shutter speed for proper exposure. The same as a light meter.

Fill-in flash—Light from a flash unit that is used to brighten shadows created by the primary light source.

Film speed—The sensitivity of a film to light, indicated by an ISO number or an exposure index (EI).

Film-speed setting—A camera setting—either manual or automatic—that tells the camera the speed of the film.

Filter—A piece of colored glass or other transparent material used over the lens to emphasize, eliminate, or change the color or density of the entire scene or certain elements in the scene.

Flash calculator dial—A control on a flash unit that tells the correct aperture for the camera-to-subject distance, or the correct distance range for a particular aperture.

Flashtube—The gas-filled tube of an electronic flash unit that emits a short, intense burst of artificial light.

COMPOSING PHOTOGRAPHS

f-number or f-stop—A number used to indicate the size of the opening on most camera lenses. Common f-numbers are f/2, f/2.8, f/4, f/5.6, f/8, f/11, f/16, and f/22. The higher the f-number, the smaller the lens opening.

Focal length—The distance from the optical center of a lens to the film plane when the lens is focused at infinity.

Freezing action—A technique that makes an object in motion appear "stopped"; can be accomplished by using a high shutter speed or electronic flash.

Frontlighting—Light that strikes the subject from the front.

Implied lines—Imaginary lines resulting from the relationship between shapes, negative spaces, and contrasts within the scene.

Intensity (or quantity) of light—A measurable quantity of light which relates to the brightness of incidental light and its affect on recorded images.

ISO speed—A system of the International Organization for Standardization for measuring film speed.

Lens—One or more pieces of optical glass or similar material designed to collect and focus rays of light to form a sharp image on film.

Manual exposure control—A camera exposure system that allows the photographer to adjust aperture and shutter speed manually.

Negative space—The space between objects in a photograph.

Normal lens—A lens that produces an image with perspective similar to that of the original scene. A normal lens "sees" the world roughly the same as our eyes do.

Off-camera flash—Using a flash unit off the camera to provide sidelighting, bounce lighting, or other directional lighting.

Overexposure—A situation in which too much light reaches the film, producing a dense negative or a light slide.

Panning—Moving the camera during exposure to follow a moving subject.

Pattern—An orderly arrangement of objects, either manmade or occurring naturally.

Point-and-shoot camera—An automatic non-SLR camera, usually with built-in flash.

Program mode—A form of exposure control in which aperture and shutter speed are selected by a computer within the camera.

Quality of light—A term referring to the harshness or softness of lighting. The other characteristics of light include color and direction.

Reflector—Any device used to reflect light onto a subject.

Reflected-light meter—An exposure meter used to measure the amount of light reflecting from a subject.

Rule of thirds—A system by which the strongest visual points in an image are determined at the four intersections made by dividing the entire frame into three equal sections, horizontally and vertically.

Selective focus—The technique of using a large lens opening to produce a shallow depth of field to isolate a subject in sharp focus from a blurred background or foreground.

Shutter-priority—A form of exposure control in which shutter speed can be selected by the photographer and the camera will adjust the aperture.

Shutter speed—The length of time that the camera shutter is open to expose the film.

Sidelighting—Light striking the subject from the side relative to the position of the camera.

Single-lens-reflex (SLR) camera—A camera that uses a prism and mirror to provide viewing through the picture-taking lens.

Stop(s)—Exposure increments. Each single-increment change in shutter speed or aperture represents one stop, and halves or doubles the amount of light striking the film. (Also see "*f*-stop.")

Telephoto lens—A lens that creates a larger image of the subject than a normal lens at the same camera-to-subject distance.

Texture—the arrangement of material as it reveals the surface of an object.

Through-the-lens meter (TTL)—A built-in camera meter that determines exposure for the scene by reading the light that passes through the lens.

Tone—The degree of lightness or darkness in any given area of a print; also referred to as value.

Tripod—A three-legged camera support with a rotating hinged head to which the camera is attached.

Tungsten-balanced film—Film that has been balanced to produce accurate color rendition under tungsten light.

Tungsten light—Light from normal household lamps and ceiling fixtures (not fluorescent).

Underexposure—A condition in which too little light reaches the film, producing a thin negative or a dark slide.

Vignetting—Darkening or lightening around the edges of an image produced by masking during printing or using a filter with a smaller diameter than that of the lens.

Visual expression—Portrayal of an idea or vision through visual means.

Wide-angle lens—A lens that covers a wider field of view than a normal lens at the same subject distance.

Zoom lens—A variable-focal-length lens that can be used in place of a number of individual fixed-focal-length lenses.

GLOSSARY

INDEX

Please note: Entries which appear in bold refer to captions.

COMPOSING PHOTOGRAPHS